Slithering Snakes

Contents	Page

written by Pam Holden

1

There are many kinds of snakes
in the world, like grass snakes,
sea snakes, and tree snakes.

They make their homes in forests, swamps, deserts, and the sea. Some snakes live in caves or rocks, and some live in trees or water.

All snakes have very long, thin bodies. The smallest snakes are only as long as your hand, but the longest ones are as long as a house!

Some kinds are as heavy as two men. The biggest snakes are so strong that they can squeeze the animals they catch.
anaconda

Snakes have no legs, so they move by sliding and slithering on the ground and on tree branches, or by swimming.

Tree snakes can jump from one tree to another. Some people think they are flying!

Some snakes have stripes or spots.
Their skins have patterns to help
them hide in grass or rocks or trees.
All snakes have scales on their skin.

8

The scales get old from sliding across the ground. Then their skin comes off in one piece. Sometimes people make it into shoes and belts and bags.

Snakes are cold-blooded, so they like to lie in the sun to get warm. Some live together in a den so they can keep warm. They sleep there in winter, when it is too cold outside. In hot deserts, they have to hide from the sun.

rattlesnakes

A snake puts its long tongue in and out
to smell food or danger. It likes to eat
the eggs of frogs, birds, and turtles.
Big snakes hunt to catch other animals.
Sometimes they eat them in one bite!

python

Most baby snakes hatch out of eggs, but other kinds are born alive. Their mothers don't look after them at all, so they have to hide from hungry birds and animals.

15

Watch out for snakes that can bite and spit poisons. Snakes hiss when they get frightened or angry. SSsssss!